# My Dog's Life

## A KEEPSAKE MEMORY BOOK

chartwell
books

# My Dog's Life

## A KEEPSAKE MEMORY BOOK

chartwell
books

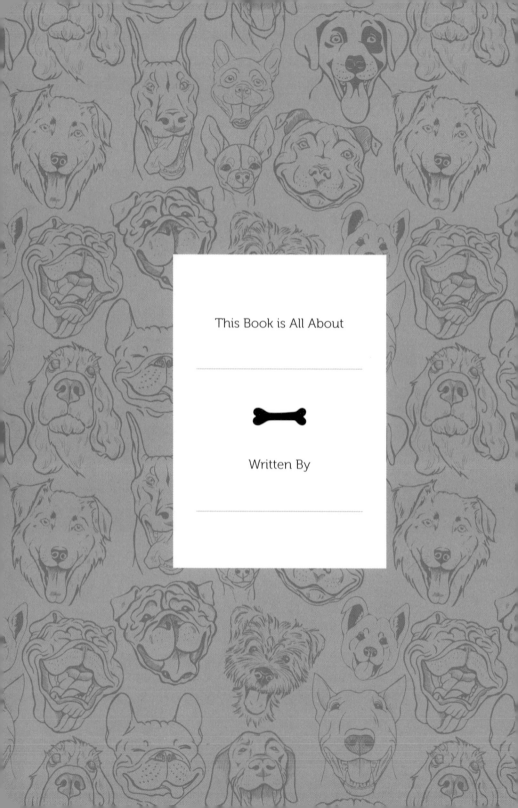

This Book is All About

_____

Written By

_____

# C●ntents

"A dog will teach you unconditional love. If you can have that in your life, things won't be too bad."

— Robert Wagner

# Introduction

Whether it's an adorable puppy or a sweet older rescue, your dog has wagged and wiggled its way into your heart and home. Use this keepsake journal to commemorate many of their dog's "firsts" (first visit to the vet, first romp at the dog park, etc.) as well as memories, mischief, and more.

Print out and paste in photos of your adorable pup to celebrate all the fun that they get up to! There's even a guestbook at the end for all your dog's new friends and admirers to fill with their favorite stories. Once you finish, you will have created a one-of-a-kind memory book that captures the magic of what makes your dog so special.

Chapter 1

# Meet Cute

The story of how you
met your dog.

**When did you start thinking about getting a dog?**

..................................................................................................
..................................................................................................
..................................................................................................
..................................................................................................
..................................................................................................
..................................................................................................
..................................................................................................
..................................................................................................

**What lead you to this decision?**

..................................................................................................
..................................................................................................
..................................................................................................
..................................................................................................
..................................................................................................
..................................................................................................
..................................................................................................
..................................................................................................
..................................................................................................
..................................................................................................
..................................................................................................
..................................................................................................

# Past Pets

**Did you own any dogs before getting this dog?**

..................................................................................................
..................................................................................................
..................................................................................................
..................................................................................................
..................................................................................................
..................................................................................................

**Did you grow up with dogs or other pets?**

..................................................................................................
..................................................................................................
..................................................................................................
..................................................................................................
..................................................................................................

**Before getting your dog, did you consider yourself a "dog person"?**

..................................................................................................
..................................................................................................
..................................................................................................
..................................................................................................
..................................................................................................

**Are there other pets in your household?**

.......................................................................................................

.......................................................................................................

.......................................................................................................

.......................................................................................................

.......................................................................................................

.......................................................................................................

.......................................................................................................

.......................................................................................................

Add some photos of
your other resident
furry, scaley, or
feathered friends.

name: _____

name: _____

**Where did you look for a dog and what research did you do?**

..........................................................................................................................

..........................................................................................................................

..........................................................................................................................

..........................................................................................................................

..........................................................................................................................

..........................................................................................................................

..........................................................................................................................

**Who did you have to convince to get a dog?**

..........................................................................................................................

..........................................................................................................................

..........................................................................................................................

..........................................................................................................................

..........................................................................................................................

..........................................................................................................................

..........................................................................................................................

**How long did you have to wait before picking up your dog?**

..........................................................................................................................

..........................................................................................................................

..........................................................................................................................

..........................................................................................................................

..........................................................................................................................

..........................................................................................................................

**Where did you get your dog?**

........................................................................................................
........................................................................................................
........................................................................................................
........................................................................................................
........................................................................................................
........................................................................................................
........................................................................................................
........................................................................................................

**Who went with you to pick your pup up?**

........................................................................................................
........................................................................................................
........................................................................................................
........................................................................................................
........................................................................................................
........................................................................................................
........................................................................................................
........................................................................................................
........................................................................................................
........................................................................................................
........................................................................................................

"Everyone thinks they have the best dog. And none of them are wrong."

– W.R. Purche

# "Before you get a dog, you can't quite imagine what living with one might be like; afterward, you can't imagine living any other way."

– Caroline Knapp

**How did you know that this dog was the right one for you?**

..........................................................................................
..........................................................................................
..........................................................................................
..........................................................................................
..........................................................................................
..........................................................................................
..........................................................................................
..........................................................................................
..........................................................................................
..........................................................................................
..........................................................................................
..........................................................................................
..........................................................................................
..........................................................................................
..........................................................................................
..........................................................................................
..........................................................................................
..........................................................................................
..........................................................................................
..........................................................................................
..........................................................................................
..........................................................................................
..........................................................................................
..........................................................................................
..........................................................................................
..........................................................................................
..........................................................................................

# Describe meeting your dog
# for the first time.

...................................................................................
...................................................................................
...................................................................................
...................................................................................
...................................................................................
...................................................................................
...................................................................................
...................................................................................
...................................................................................
...................................................................................
...................................................................................
...................................................................................
...................................................................................
...................................................................................
...................................................................................
...................................................................................
...................................................................................
...................................................................................
...................................................................................

**How did your dog's first RIDE in the CAR go?**

....................................................................................................
....................................................................................................
....................................................................................................
....................................................................................................
....................................................................................................
....................................................................................................
....................................................................................................
....................................................................................................
....................................................................................................
....................................................................................................
....................................................................................................
....................................................................................................
....................................................................................................
....................................................................................................
....................................................................................................
....................................................................................................
....................................................................................................
....................................................................................................
....................................................................................................
....................................................................................................
....................................................................................................
....................................................................................................
....................................................................................................
....................................................................................................
....................................................................................................

# "You can trust your dog to guard your house but never trust your dog to guard your sandwich."

—Unknown

**How did your dog react to their new home?**

...........................................................................................
...........................................................................................
...........................................................................................
...........................................................................................
...........................................................................................
...........................................................................................
...........................................................................................
...........................................................................................
...........................................................................................
...........................................................................................
...........................................................................................

**How did the first night go?**

...........................................................................................
...........................................................................................
...........................................................................................
...........................................................................................
...........................................................................................
...........................................................................................
...........................................................................................
...........................................................................................
...........................................................................................
...........................................................................................

**Where did your dog sleep the first night?**

..................................................................................................................
..................................................................................................................
..................................................................................................................
..................................................................................................................
..................................................................................................................
..................................................................................................................
..................................................................................................................

z-z-z

**Where does your dog sleep now?**

..................................................................................................................
..................................................................................................................
..................................................................................................................
..................................................................................................................
..................................................................................................................
..................................................................................................................
..................................................................................................................

**List the supplies you bought in preparation for your pup's arrival:**

**New homecoming or "puppy shower" gifts from friends:**

from: _____          from: _____

gift: _____          gift: _____

_____          _____


from: _____          from: _____

gift: _____          gift: _____

_____          _____


from: _____          from: _____

gift: _____          gift: _____

_____          _____


from: _____          from: _____

gift: _____          gift: _____

_____          _____


from: _____          from: _____

gift: _____          gift: _____

_____          _____


from: _____          from: _____

gift: _____          gift: _____

_____          _____

# I love my new toys and treats!

Woof Woof

date: _____

**These are my favorite toys:**     **Toys I want:**

How did you "puppy-proof" your home
and get it ready for your new dog?

........................................................
........................................................
........................................................
........................................................
........................................................
........................................................
........................................................
........................................................
........................................................
........................................................
........................................................
........................................................
........................................................

On a scale of **1-10**, how
prepared were you
for your dog's arrival?
*(circle a number)*

**1** **2** **3** **4** **5**

**6** **7** **8** **9** **10**

........................................................
........................................................
........................................................
........................................................
........................................................
........................................................
........................................................

**What did you wish you had done (or not done) before bringing your pup home? Any items you were missing?**

# Chapter 2

# All About You!

All the Facts About
Your Favorite Pup

# What's in a Name

**What is your dog's name?**

..................................................................................................................

**Who came up with that name? What inspired it?**

..................................................................................................
..................................................................................................
..................................................................................................
..................................................................................................
..................................................................................................
..................................................................................................
..................................................................................................
..................................................................................................

**Does your dog have a middle name? If so, what is it?**

..................................................................................................................

**What other names did you consider?**

write the names
on the tags

# Top 10
## Most Popular
# Male
## Dog Names

**#1**
Max

**#2**
Charlie

**#3**
Cooper

**#4**
Buddy

**#5**
Milo

**#6**
Bear

**#7**
Rocky

**#8**
Duke

**#9**
Tucker

**#10**
Jack

# Top 10
## Most Popular
# Female
## Dog Names

**#1**
Bella

**#2**
Luna

**#3**
Lucy

**#4**
Daisy

**#5**
Zoe

**#6**
Lily

**#7**
Lola

**#8**
Bailey

**#9**
Stella

**#10**
Molly

# Top 50 Most Popular
# **Dog Breeds** in America

1. Retrievers (Labrador)
2. French Bulldogs
3. Retrievers (Golden)
4. German Shepherd Dogs
5. Poodles
6. Bulldogs
7. Beagles
8. Rottweilers
9. Pointers (German Shorthaired)
10. Dachshunds
11. Pembroke Welsh Corgis
12. Australian Shepherds
13. Yorkshire Terriers
14. Boxers
15. Cavalier King Charles Spaniels
16. Doberman Pinschers
17. Great Danes
18. Miniature Schnauzers
19. Siberian Huskies
20. Bernese Mountain Dogs
21. Cane Corso
22. Shih Tzu
23. Boston Terriers
24. Pomeranians
25. Havanese
26. Spaniels (English Springer)
27. Brittanys
28. Shetland Sheepdogs
29. Spaniels (Cocker)
30. Miniature American Shepherds
31. Border Collies
32. Vizslas
33. Pugs
34. Basset Hounds
35. Mastiffs
36. Belgian Malinois
37. Chihuahuas
38. Collies
39. Maltese
40. Weimaraners
41. Rhodesian Ridgebacks
42. Shiba Inu
43. Spaniels (English Cocker)
44. Portuguese Water Dogs
45. Newfoundlands
46. West Highland White Terriers
47. Bichons Frises
48. Retrievers (Chesapeake Bay)
49. Dalmatians
50. Bloodhounds

#28

#16

#2

Does your pup make the list?

#33

#19

#39

# Give Us the Deets

**What breed (or breed mix) is your dog?**

_____

_____

_____

**What color is your dog?**

_____

_____

**What type of hair does your dog have?**

_____

_____

**Ears up or down?**

_____

**Long tail or short?**

_____

**Long nose or short?**

_____

**Is your dog's build small, medium, or large?**

_____

**Eye color?**

_____

**How would you describe how your dog looks to a stranger?**

..............................................................................................................
..............................................................................................................
..............................................................................................................
..............................................................................................................
..............................................................................................................
..............................................................................................................

**Which of your dog's physical attributes do you think are the most adorable?**

..............................................................................................................
..............................................................................................................
..............................................................................................................
..............................................................................................................
..............................................................................................................
..............................................................................................................
..............................................................................................................
..............................................................................................................
..............................................................................................................
..............................................................................................................
..............................................................................................................
..............................................................................................................
..............................................................................................................
..............................................................................................................
..............................................................................................................

# The Name Game

Dogs seem to collect nicknames. And these pet names (no pun intended) have a funny way of evolving! **Trace the evolution of some of your favorite nicknames for your dog. Ex. A dog named Honey: Honey Bun •----> Honey Bunch •----> Honey Bunches of Oats •----> Oats**

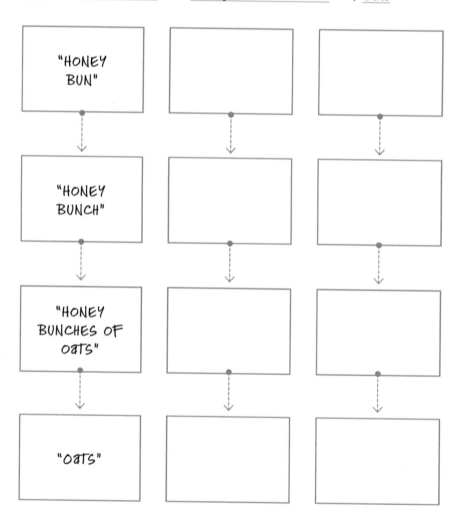

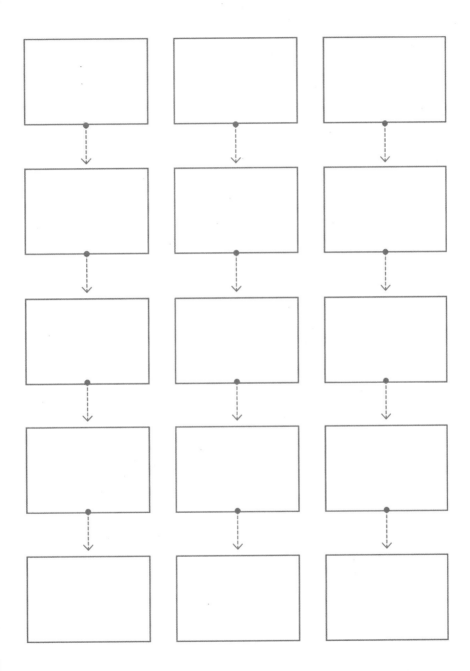

## Chapter 3

# There's a First Time for Everything

Whether you're bringing home a newly weaned puppy or a full-grown rescue, you'll want to commemorate all fido's firsts.

**How old is your dog today?**

..................................................................................................

**When is your dog's birthday or Gotcha Day?**

..................................................................................................

Here's a photo on Gotcha Day

date:

**Who were the first people in your household to meet the dog, and how did that go?**

..................................................................................................
..................................................................................................
..................................................................................................
..................................................................................................
..................................................................................................

**If there are other animals in the house, how did that meeting go?**

..................................................................................................
..................................................................................................
..................................................................................................
..................................................................................................
..................................................................................................

**What happened the first time your dog responded to their name?**

**What was the first toy you bought your dog?**

...................................................................................................

...................................................................................................

...................................................................................................

...................................................................................................

...................................................................................................

...................................................................................................

...................................................................................................

...................................................................................................

...................................................................................................

...................................................................................................

...................................................................................................

...................................................................................................

...................................................................................................

...................................................................................................

...................................................................................................

...................................................................................................

...................................................................................................

...................................................................................................

## "The dog lives for the day, the hour, even the moment."

– Robert Falcon Scott

**What was your dog's first command they mastered?**

..............................................................................................
..............................................................................................
..............................................................................................
..............................................................................................
..............................................................................................
..............................................................................................
..............................................................................................
..............................................................................................
..............................................................................................
..............................................................................................

**What was your dog's first trick and how did you train them to do it?**

..............................................................................................
..............................................................................................
..............................................................................................
..............................................................................................
..............................................................................................
..............................................................................................
..............................................................................................
..............................................................................................
..............................................................................................
..............................................................................................
..............................................................................................
..............................................................................................
..............................................................................................

# "Dogs do speak, but only to those who know how to listen."

– Orhan Pamuk

**What was your dog's reaction the first time they saw snow?**

**What was your dog's reaction the first time you took them out in the rain?**

..........................................................................................................

..........................................................................................................

..........................................................................................................

..........................................................................................................

..........................................................................................................

..........................................................................................................

..........................................................................................................

..........................................................................................................

..........................................................................................................

..........................................................................................................

..........................................................................................................

..........................................................................................................

..........................................................................................................

**What happened the first time your dog tried to take the stairs?**

..........................................................................................................

..........................................................................................................

..........................................................................................................

..........................................................................................................

..........................................................................................................

..........................................................................................................

..........................................................................................................

..........................................................................................................

..........................................................................................................

..........................................................................................................

**What was your dog's reaction when you first put on their collar?**

..................................................................................................
..................................................................................................
..................................................................................................
..................................................................................................
..................................................................................................
..................................................................................................
..................................................................................................
..................................................................................................
..................................................................................................
..................................................................................................
..................................................................................................
..................................................................................................

**What happened on your first walk together?**

........................................................................................
........................................................................................
........................................................................................
........................................................................................
........................................................................................
........................................................................................
........................................................................................
........................................................................................
........................................................................................
........................................................................................
........................................................................................
........................................................................................
........................................................................................
........................................................................................
........................................................................................
........................................................................................
........................................................................................
........................................................................................
........................................................................................
........................................................................................
........................................................................................
........................................................................................
........................................................................................
........................................................................................
........................................................................................
........................................................................................

**If you've been to a dog park, where was it and what happened the first time there?**

...................................................................................................

...................................................................................................

...................................................................................................

...................................................................................................

...................................................................................................

...................................................................................................

...................................................................................................

...................................................................................................

...................................................................................................

...................................................................................................

...................................................................................................

...................................................................................................

...................................................................................................

...................................................................................................

# Meet the Pack

Here's a few of our dog park friends.

name:

name:

name:

name:

"Fall in love with a dog, and in many ways you enter a new orbit, a universe that features not just new colors but new rituals, new rules, a new way of experiencing attachment."

– Caroline Knapp

**The first time your dog saw a river/the beach/a pool/other body of water, what happened?**

..........................................................................................
..........................................................................................
..........................................................................................
..........................................................................................
..........................................................................................
..........................................................................................
..........................................................................................
..........................................................................................

**If your dog swims, what happened the first time?**

..........................................................................................
..........................................................................................
..........................................................................................
..........................................................................................
..........................................................................................
..........................................................................................
..........................................................................................
..........................................................................................
..........................................................................................
..........................................................................................
..........................................................................................
..........................................................................................
..........................................................................................
..........................................................................................
..........................................................................................

**What are some of the first foods your dog tried (either puppy/dog food or table food they snitched)?**

**What was your dog's first veterinarian experience like? Who was the vet?**

..............................................................................................
..............................................................................................
..............................................................................................
..............................................................................................
..............................................................................................
..............................................................................................
..............................................................................................
..............................................................................................
..............................................................................................
..............................................................................................
..............................................................................................
..............................................................................................
..............................................................................................
..............................................................................................
..............................................................................................
..............................................................................................
..............................................................................................
..............................................................................................
..............................................................................................
..............................................................................................
..............................................................................................
..............................................................................................
..............................................................................................
..............................................................................................
..............................................................................................
..............................................................................................

**What was your dog's reaction to getting their nails trimmed for the first time? Did you do it, or did you have someone else do it?**

................................................................................................

................................................................................................

................................................................................................

................................................................................................

................................................................................................

................................................................................................

................................................................................................

................................................................................................

................................................................................................

................................................................................................

................................................................................................

................................................................................................

................................................................................................

................................................................................................

................................................................................................

**Describe what happened the first time your dog went to the groomer or had their first bath.**

.......................................................................................................................
.......................................................................................................................
.......................................................................................................................
.......................................................................................................................
.......................................................................................................................
.......................................................................................................................
.......................................................................................................................
.......................................................................................................................
.......................................................................................................................
.......................................................................................................................
.......................................................................................................................
.......................................................................................................................
.......................................................................................................................
.......................................................................................................................
.......................................................................................................................
.......................................................................................................................
.......................................................................................................................
.......................................................................................................................
.......................................................................................................................
.......................................................................................................................
.......................................................................................................................
.......................................................................................................................
.......................................................................................................................
.......................................................................................................................

**What happened the first time you tried putting clothes or a costume on your dog?**

**What was it, and how did your dog react?**

........................................................................................
........................................................................................
........................................................................................
........................................................................................
........................................................................................
........................................................................................
........................................................................................
........................................................................................
........................................................................................
........................................................................................
........................................................................................
........................................................................................
........................................................................................
........................................................................................
........................................................................................
........................................................................................
........................................................................................
........................................................................................
........................................................................................
........................................................................................
........................................................................................
........................................................................................
........................................................................................
........................................................................................
........................................................................................
........................................................................................
........................................................................................
........................................................................................

"It is amazing how much love and laughter [dogs] bring into our lives and even how much closer we become with each other because of them."

– John Grogan

**If your dog has been to obedience classes, describe that first class. Where was it, what kind of other dogs were there, how did your dog do?**

..................................................................................................................
..................................................................................................................
..................................................................................................................
..................................................................................................................
..................................................................................................................
..................................................................................................................
..................................................................................................................
..................................................................................................................
..................................................................................................................
..................................................................................................................
..................................................................................................................
..................................................................................................................
..................................................................................................................
..................................................................................................................
..................................................................................................................
..................................................................................................................
..................................................................................................................
..................................................................................................................
..................................................................................................................
..................................................................................................................
..................................................................................................................
..................................................................................................................
..................................................................................................................
..................................................................................................................

# Chapter 4

# A Few of Your Pup's Favorite Things

What really makes
their tail wag?

**What is your dog's favorite meal? Special treat?**

....................................................................................................

....................................................................................................

....................................................................................................

....................................................................................................

....................................................................................................

....................................................................................................

....................................................................................................

....................................................................................................

....................................................................................................

....................................................................................................

**Do you feed them any human food? What is their best begging tactic?**

....................................................................................................

....................................................................................................

....................................................................................................

....................................................................................................

....................................................................................................

....................................................................................................

....................................................................................................

....................................................................................................

....................................................................................................

....................................................................................................

....................................................................................................

....................................................................................................

....................................................................................................

....................................................................................................

**Who is your dog's favorite person that's not you?**

.......................................................................................
.......................................................................................
.......................................................................................
.......................................................................................
.......................................................................................
.......................................................................................
.......................................................................................
.......................................................................................
.......................................................................................
.......................................................................................

**How can you tell?**

.......................................................................................
.......................................................................................
.......................................................................................
.......................................................................................
.......................................................................................
.......................................................................................
.......................................................................................
.......................................................................................
.......................................................................................
.......................................................................................
.......................................................................................
.......................................................................................
.......................................................................................
.......................................................................................

**"Dogs have given us their absolute all. We are the center of their universe. We are the focus of their love and faith and trust. They serve us in return for scraps. It is without a doubt the best deal man has ever made."**

– Roger A. Caras

**What's your dog's favorite place to nap?**

........................................................................
........................................................................
........................................................................
........................................................................
........................................................................
........................................................................
........................................................................
........................................................................
........................................................................
........................................................................

**What's your dog's favorite place to be scratched?**

........................................................................
........................................................................
........................................................................
........................................................................
........................................................................
........................................................................
........................................................................
........................................................................
........................................................................
........................................................................
........................................................................

**What's your dog's favorite thing to watch out the window?**

..............................................
..............................................
..............................................
..............................................
..............................................
..............................................
...........................................................................
...........................................................................
...........................................................................
...........................................................................
...........................................................................
...........................................................................

**What's your dog's favorite thing to have playing on the tv or radio?**

...........................................................................
...........................................................................
...........................................................................
...........................................................................
...........................................................................
...........................................................................
...........................................................................
...........................................................................

**What's your dog's favorite way to greet family and visitors?**

..................................................................................................
..................................................................................................
..................................................................................................
..................................................................................................
..................................................................................................
..................................................................................................
..................................................................................................
..................................................................................................
..................................................................................................
..................................................................................................
..................................................................................................
..................................................................................................
..................................................................................................
..................................................................................................
..................................................................................................
..................................................................................................
..................................................................................................
..................................................................................................
..................................................................................................

# "Happiness is coming home and knowing your dog is there to greet you."

**What's your dog's favorite walking route/destination?**

..............................................................................................................
..............................................................................................................
..............................................................................................................
..............................................................................................................
..............................................................................................................
..............................................................................................................
..............................................................................................................
..............................................................................................................
..............................................................................................................
..............................................................................................................
..............................................................................................................

**What are their favorite things to sniff?**

..............................................................................................................
..............................................................................................................
..............................................................................................................
..............................................................................................................
..............................................................................................................
..............................................................................................................
..............................................................................................................
..............................................................................................................
..............................................................................................................
..............................................................................................................

**What's your dog's favorite outdoor activity?**

..........................................................................................
..........................................................................................
..........................................................................................
..........................................................................................
..........................................................................................
..........................................................................................
..........................................................................................
..........................................................................................
..........................................................................................
..........................................................................................
..........................................................................................
..........................................................................................

**What is your dog's favorite indoor activity?**

..........................................................................................
..........................................................................................
..........................................................................................
..........................................................................................
..........................................................................................
..........................................................................................
..........................................................................................
..........................................................................................
..........................................................................................
..........................................................................................
..........................................................................................
..........................................................................................

# Canine Influencer

Does your dog have their own Instagram or TikTok account?
What do they post? Who follows them?

"A dog is one of the remaining reasons why some people can be persuaded to go for a walk."

—Orlando Aloysius Battista

**What's your dog's favorite thing to "steal"?**

....................................................................................................
....................................................................................................
....................................................................................................
....................................................................................................
....................................................................................................
....................................................................................................
....................................................................................................
....................................................................................................
....................................................................................................
....................................................................................................
....................................................................................................

**Where is your dog's favorite place to hide things?**

....................................................................................................
....................................................................................................
....................................................................................................
....................................................................................................
....................................................................................................
....................................................................................................
....................................................................................................
....................................................................................................
....................................................................................................
....................................................................................................
....................................................................................................

**What's your dog's favorite game to play with other dogs?**

................................................................................
................................................................................
................................................................................
................................................................................
................................................................................
................................................................................
................................................................................
................................................................................
................................................................................
................................................................................

**What's your dog's favorite game to play with humans?**

................................................................................
................................................................................
................................................................................
................................................................................
................................................................................
................................................................................
................................................................................
................................................................................
................................................................................
................................................................................
................................................................................
................................................................................

# Chapter 5

# Pet Peeves

Even the most happy-go-lucky dog can have some picky puppy preferences.

**What toy did you give your dog that they hated, feared, or otherwise wanted nothing to do with?**

......................................................................................................
......................................................................................................
......................................................................................................
......................................................................................................
......................................................................................................
......................................................................................................
......................................................................................................
......................................................................................................
......................................................................................................
......................................................................................................

**Are there typical doggie games that your dog would rather not do, like Frisbees, agility courses, or fetch?**

......................................................................................................
......................................................................................................
......................................................................................................
......................................................................................................
......................................................................................................
......................................................................................................
......................................................................................................
......................................................................................................
......................................................................................................
......................................................................................................
......................................................................................................
......................................................................................................

**What's your dog's worst mode of transportation?**
**Do they get carsick? Do they like the windows up or down?**

........................................................................................
........................................................................................
........................................................................................
........................................................................................
........................................................................................
........................................................................................
........................................................................................
........................................................................................
........................................................................................
........................................................................................
........................................................................................
........................................................................................
........................................................................................
........................................................................................
........................................................................................
........................................................................................
........................................................................................
........................................................................................
........................................................................................
........................................................................................
........................................................................................
........................................................................................
........................................................................................
........................................................................................

# "Some of our greatest historical and artistic treasures we place with curators in museums; others we take for walks."

—Roger Caras

What's your dog's attitude towards walks? Love them so much you have to spell out the word to keep them from getting too excited? Or dislike walks so much they protest by plopping themselves down on a street corner?

......................................................................................................................

......................................................................................................................

......................................................................................................................

......................................................................................................................

......................................................................................................................

......................................................................................................................

......................................................................................................................

......................................................................................................................

......................................................................................................................

......................................................................................................................

......................................................................................................................

......................................................................................................................

......................................................................................................................

......................................................................................................................

......................................................................................................................

......................................................................................................................

......................................................................................................................

......................................................................................................................

......................................................................................................................

......................................................................................................................

......................................................................................................................

......................................................................................................................

......................................................................................................................

blech!

**What food(s) does your dog turn his nose up at?**

What everyday household activities sends your dog running (e.g., vacuuming, grinding coffee, turning on the oven [because it sets off the fire alarm], turning on fans?

........................................................................................

........................................................................................

........................................................................................

........................................................................................

........................................................................................

........................................................................................

........................................................................................

........................................................................................

........................................................................................

........................................................................................

........................................................................................

........................................................................................

........................................................................................

........................................................................................

........................................................................................

........................................................................................

........................................................................................

........................................................................................

........................................................................................

........................................................................................

........................................................................................

........................................................................................

........................................................................................

........................................................................................

........................................................................................

**What neighborhood animals does your dog hate or fear (e.g., squirrels, the neighbor's cat, birds at the feeder, other dogs)?**

....................................................................................................
....................................................................................................
....................................................................................................
....................................................................................................
....................................................................................................
....................................................................................................
....................................................................................................
....................................................................................................
....................................................................................................
....................................................................................................
....................................................................................................
....................................................................................................
....................................................................................................
....................................................................................................
....................................................................................................
....................................................................................................
....................................................................................................
....................................................................................................
....................................................................................................
....................................................................................................
....................................................................................................

# "Anybody who doesn't know what soap tastes like, never washed a dog."

—Franklin P. Jones

**How do you give your dog medicine? Are there specific antics they do once you get a pill in their mouth?**

......................................................................................................

......................................................................................................

......................................................................................................

......................................................................................................

......................................................................................................

......................................................................................................

......................................................................................................

......................................................................................................

......................................................................................................

......................................................................................................

**How does your dog behave at the vet?**

......................................................................................................

......................................................................................................

......................................................................................................

......................................................................................................

......................................................................................................

......................................................................................................

......................................................................................................

......................................................................................................

......................................................................................................

......................................................................................................

......................................................................................................

**What body part does your dog not like you messing with (e.g., cleaning ears, cleansing facial folds, brushing teeth, trimming toenails, clipping bangs, pats on the head, scratches under the chin, wiping their behind)?**

..................................................................................................
..................................................................................................
..................................................................................................
..................................................................................................
..................................................................................................
..................................................................................................
..................................................................................................
..................................................................................................
..................................................................................................
..................................................................................................
..................................................................................................
..................................................................................................
..................................................................................................
..................................................................................................
..................................................................................................
..................................................................................................
..................................................................................................
..................................................................................................
..................................................................................................
..................................................................................................
..................................................................................................
..................................................................................................
..................................................................................................
..................................................................................................
..................................................................................................
..................................................................................................

"Dogs teach
us a very
important
lesson in life:
the mailman
is not to
be trusted."

—Sian Ford

**What are some seemingly irrational things your dog dislikes? For example, the garbage in one specific room, the look of a whole watermelon, their shadow, paper grocery bags, a throw pillow on the couch...**

.......................................................................

.......................................................................

.......................................................................

.......................................................................

.......................................................................

.......................................................................

.......................................................................

.......................................................................

.......................................................................

.......................................................................

.......................................................................

.......................................................................

.......................................................................

.......................................................................

.......................................................................

.......................................................................

.......................................................................

.......................................................................

.......................................................................

.......................................................................

.......................................................................

**What concessions do you make for some of these odd dislikes and phobias? (i.e. how well has your dog got you trained?)**

..................................................................................................
..................................................................................................
..................................................................................................
..................................................................................................
..................................................................................................
..................................................................................................
..................................................................................................
..................................................................................................
..................................................................................................
..................................................................................................
..................................................................................................
..................................................................................................
..................................................................................................
..................................................................................................
..................................................................................................
..................................................................................................

## "Properly trained, a man can be dog's best friend."

—Corey Ford

**Which visitors does your dog particularly dislike (e.g., your aunt, the neighbor kid, the pizza guy, anyone in uniform), and what do they do to show their dislike?**

WOOOF
WOOOF
WOOOF

Where do you suspect is your dog's favorite comfy spot
when you're not looking—a certain couch, chair, or bed, perhaps?
What do they do when you catch them on it?

......................................................................................

......................................................................................

......................................................................................

......................................................................................

......................................................................................

......................................................................................

......................................................................................

......................................................................................

......................................................................................

......................................................................................

......................................................................................

......................................................................................

......................................................................................

......................................................................................

......................................................................................

## "No home decor is complete without dog hair."

**What's your dog's least favorite accessory? The Christmas sweater? The Halloween costume? The bow-tie or tutu? The rain booties?**

**Even when you're home, you dog can still become bored. What are some things they do to get your attention?**

......................................................................................
......................................................................................
......................................................................................
......................................................................................
......................................................................................
......................................................................................
......................................................................................
......................................................................................
......................................................................................
......................................................................................
......................................................................................
......................................................................................
......................................................................................
......................................................................................
......................................................................................
......................................................................................
......................................................................................
......................................................................................
......................................................................................
......................................................................................
......................................................................................
......................................................................................
......................................................................................
......................................................................................
......................................................................................

# "Scratch a dog and you'll find a permanent job"

—Franklin Jones

Your dog's biggest pet peeve is you leaving, as you are their favorite person in the whole world. What do you think they're feeling when you walk out the door?

........................................................................................

........................................................................................

........................................................................................

........................................................................................

........................................................................................

........................................................................................

........................................................................................

........................................................................................

........................................................................................

........................................................................................

........................................................................................

.............................                         ............................

.............................                         ............................

.............................                         ............................

.............................                         ............................

# "A dog is the only thing on earth that loves you more than he loves himself."

—Josh Billings

**What do you think they do (or, what have you seen them do, if you have a doggie-cam)?**

...................................................................................................

...................................................................................................

...................................................................................................

...................................................................................................

...................................................................................................

...................................................................................................

...................................................................................................

...................................................................................................

...................................................................................................

**What's the worst thing they've done?**

...................................................................................................

...................................................................................................

...................................................................................................

...................................................................................................

...................................................................................................

...................................................................................................

...................................................................................................

...................................................................................................

...................................................................................................

...................................................................................................

...................................................................................................

...................................................................................................

# Party Foul!

In a 2022 Newsweek poll, 25% of pet owners reported feeling frustrated with their pets from time to time. It's okay to be bothered by things your dog does—it happens to all roommates from time to time!—just so long as you're not punishing your dog for these behaviors, instead working on redirecting and training them to do better.

**Here are a sample of things that might get under your skin.**

\_\_\_\_\_ **Pulling toilet paper off the roll.**

\_\_\_\_\_ **Laying atop all the bed covers so you can't pull them up.**

\_\_\_\_\_ **Tearing apart new stuffies within minutes.**

\_\_\_\_\_ **Tearing apart things that aren't new stuffies.**

\_\_\_\_\_ **Going after presents (under the Christmas or hiding behind furniture).**

\_\_\_\_\_ **Sniffing everything before finding just the right spot to do their business while on a walk.**

\_\_\_\_\_ **Hiding one of your shoes.**

\_\_\_\_\_ **Digging in your garden or yard.**

\_\_\_\_\_ **Following you around the house/getting under your feet.**

\_\_\_\_\_ **Farting while lying at your feet.**

**Write about some other doggie *faux paws*.**

_____

_____

_____

_____

_____

_____

_____

_____

_____

_____

_____

# Et tu, person?

Here are some pet peeves your dog might have about you. Check off any that apply to your dog (and your own behavior), include any others, then write about some of the funnier moments.

_____ You yell at your dog for barking.

_____ You go on a power walk or quick walk and not let your dog sniff all the smells.

_____ You blame your farts on the dog.

_____ You spray cleaners, perfume/cologne, or anything heavily scented near them.

_____ You fake a throw for fetch.

_____ You come home smelling of other dogs.

_____ You hug their neck for too long or give too many kisses in the face.

_____ You go in the car without them.

_____ You ignore them when they're being good and/or only give consistent attention when they're getting into mischief.

_____ You cooked bacon and didn't give them any.

_____ _____

_____ _____

_____ _____

_____ _____

_____ _____

**Such short little lives our pets have to spend with us, and they spend most of it watching for us to come home each day."**

– John Grogan

Chapter 6

# Everyday Fun

More fun than the
major milestones, the joy of
living with your dog
lies in the daily details.

**Write about a typical day in your dog's life.**

# 100%
## of respondents to a Glamour magazine poll reported that they've said
# "I love you"
## to their dog.

# "Dogs leave pawprints on our hearts"

– Author Unknown

If there were a movie about your dog, who would be the voice of your dog?

.................................................

.................................................

.................................................

.................................................

.................................................

.................................................

.................................................

Would the movie be action, adventure, comedy, drama?

.................................................................................

.................................................................................

.................................................................................

.................................................................................

.................................................................................

.................................................................................

.................................................................................

.................................................................................

.................................................................................

.................................................................................

.................................................................................

# Let's Talk

In 2021, researchers from the Department of Psychology and Neuroscience at Dalhousie University in Nova Scotia, Canada, concluded that dogs can understand 89 spoken words, on average—which is about the same as an 18-month-old child. In addition to the words you specifically use for their toys and other everyday items or events, here are a few general words they know:

**Circle which words you know your dog understands.**

| | | |
|---|---|---|
| Bath | Park | Sit |
| Vet | Good boy/ | Watch |
| Walk | girl | Heel |
| Treat | Come | No |
| Water | Down | Okay |
| Ride | Stay | Leave it |
| | Wait | |

**What are some other words your dog knows?**

"**Money can buy you a fine dog, but only love can make him wag his tail.**"

– Kinky Friedman

**What are your terms of endearment for your dog?**

_____   _____

_____   _____

_____   _____

_____   _____

_____   _____

_____   _____


**Does each member of your family have a preferred nickname for your dog?**

name:

nickname:

name:

nickname:

name:

nickname:

name:

nickname:

name:

nickname:

name:

nickname:

**Try this:**

Try reading your dog a story and see how they react. Get cozy, down to their level, and just start reading. Don't hold back from doing *alllll* the voices! Here are some you might try:

**101 Dalmatians**
by Dodie Smith

**Lady and the Tramp**

**Marley and Me**
by John Grogan

**White Fang**
by Jack London

**The Call of the Wild**
by Jack London

**Greyfriars Bobby**
by Eleanor Atkinson

**The Curious Incident of the Dog in the Night-Time**
by Mark Haddon

**Flush**
by Virginia Woolf

**A Dog's Purpose**
by W. Bruce Cameron

**"Mercy & Elvis"**
**mysteries series**
by Paula Munier

**Henry the Queen's Corgi**
by Georgie Crawley

**Rescue and Jessica**
by Jessica Kensky
and Patrick Downes

**The Dog Who Wouldn't Be**
by Farley Mowat

**Jake the Growling Dog**
by Samantha Shannon

**Wish**
by Barbara O'Connor

**Dog**
by Shaun Tan

**"A Dog's Tale"**
by Mark Twain

**"Memoirs of a Yellow Dog"**
by O. Henry

**"Investigations of a Dog"**
by Franz Kafka

**"Roog"**
by Philip K. Dick

**What have you read to your dog, and how did they react?**

............................................................................................
............................................................................................
............................................................................................
............................................................................................
............................................................................................
............................................................................................
............................................................................................
............................................................................................
............................................................................................
............................................................................................
............................................................................................
............................................................................................
............................................................................................
............................................................................................
............................................................................................
............................................................................................
............................................................................................
............................................................................................
............................................................................................
............................................................................................

# Party Animal!

Throw your dog a birthday (or gotcha day) party. You don't have to throw a divine shindig the likes of King Louis XIV, with live chess pieces and fountains of wine. In fact, all your dog wants is your attention.

**How did you celebrate your dog's birthday or gotcha day? Who was there?**

......................................................................................

......................................................................................

......................................................................................

......................................................................................

......................................................................................

......................................................................................

......................................................................................

......................................................................................

......................................................................................

......................................................................................

......................................................................................

......................................................................................

......................................................................................

......................................................................................

......................................................................................

......................................................................................

**What was something special or out of the ordinary you did together?**

..............................................................................

..............................................................................

..............................................................................

..............................................................................

..............................................................................

..............................................................................

..............................................................................

..............................................................................

..............................................................................

..............................................................................

**What did your dog eat for their special day?**

..............................................................................

..............................................................................

..............................................................................

..............................................................................

..............................................................................

..............................................................................

..............................................................................

..............................................................................

..............................................................................

..............................................................................

**Try this:**

Wink at your dog. Better yet: catch their gaze, do a deliberately exaggerated wink, and say "Wink?" in the voice your doggo likes best. Try this a few times and see if your partner in crime winks back when you say the word.

**What happens when you wink at your dog?**
**After practicing, do they wink back?**

........................................................................................................

........................................................................................................

........................................................................................................

........................................................................................................

........................................................................................................

........................................................................................................

........................................................................................................

........................................................................................................

........................................................................................................

........................................................................................................

**Try this:**
Play peek-a-boo with your dog. Do it a few times, then try gently covering your dog's face for just a moment before removing it with a mellow "peek-a-boo!"

**How does your dog react?**

.............................................................................................................
.............................................................................................................
.............................................................................................................
.............................................................................................................
.............................................................................................................
.............................................................................................................
.............................................................................................................

**Are there other silly games you play with your dog?**

.............................................................................................................
.............................................................................................................
.............................................................................................................
.............................................................................................................
.............................................................................................................
.............................................................................................................
.............................................................................................................
.............................................................................................................
.............................................................................................................

What sets your dog off on the zoomies (or other show of excitement)? For example, the theme to your favorite late-night talk show, every time you open the basement door, when you pull clothes out of the dryer or when they "survive" their bath...

......................................................................................................

......................................................................................................

......................................................................................................

......................................................................................................

......................................................................................................

......................................................................................................

......................................................................................................

......................................................................................................

......................................................................................................

......................................................................................................

......................................................................................................

......................................................................................................

......................................................................................................

......................................................................................................

......................................................................................................

......................................................................................................

......................................................................................................

......................................................................................................

......................................................................................................

**What does your dog bark at on television (e.g., horses, birds, cartoon voices)?**

................................................................................................

................................................................................................

................................................................................................

................................................................................................

................................................................................................

................................................................................................

................................................................................................

................................................................................................

................................................................................................

................................................................................................

................................................................................................

................................................................................................

................................................................................................

................................................................................................

Arf
Arf

## "Even the tiniest Poodle or Chihuahua is still a wolf at heart."

– Dorothy Hinshaw

**Write about your favorite road trip or vacation you have taken with your dog.**

......................................................................................................
......................................................................................................
......................................................................................................
......................................................................................................
......................................................................................................
......................................................................................................
......................................................................................................
......................................................................................................
......................................................................................................

**Where did you go?**

......................................................................................................
......................................................................................................
......................................................................................................
......................................................................................................
......................................................................................................
......................................................................................................
......................................................................................................
......................................................................................................
......................................................................................................
......................................................................................................
......................................................................................................

**What was your favorite part?**

.......................................................................................
.......................................................................................
.......................................................................................
.......................................................................................
.......................................................................................
.......................................................................................
.......................................................................................
.......................................................................................
.......................................................................................
.......................................................................................
.......................................................................................

**What was their favorite part?**

.......................................................................................
.......................................................................................
.......................................................................................
.......................................................................................
.......................................................................................
.......................................................................................
.......................................................................................
.......................................................................................
.......................................................................................
.......................................................................................
.......................................................................................
.......................................................................................
.......................................................................................

**Here are some of the best pictures from the trip.**

date: _____
_____

date: _____
_____
_____
_____
_____
_____

date:

**What are some things your dog does that always makes you laugh?**

.......................................................................................
.......................................................................................
.......................................................................................
.......................................................................................
.......................................................................................
.......................................................................................
.......................................................................................
.......................................................................................
.......................................................................................
.......................................................................................
.......................................................................................
.......................................................................................
.......................................................................................
.......................................................................................
.......................................................................................
.......................................................................................

# "The great pleasure of a dog is that you may make a fool of yourself with him and not only will he not scold you, but he will make a fool of himself too."

— Samuel Butler

# Barks and Crafts!

Let your pup be your muse and inspire your creative side! Give these artistic activities a go. Ignore your inner critic, after all, your dog will think everything you make is fantastic!

**Sketch a portrait of your dog.**

**Write a poem, limerick, or jingle inspired by your dog.**

# Your Dog's Paw Print!

**Instructions:**
Grab some water-based, non-toxic paint or ink and dip your dog's paw into the paint. Then gently press the paw onto this page for a couple seconds before lifting the paw straight up from the page to avoid smudging. Wash and clean your pup's paw right away.

place paw here

"Petting, scratching, and cuddling a dog could be as soothing to the mind and heart as deep meditation and almost as good for the soul as prayer."

– Dean Koontz

**How does your dog turn on the charm? Has your dog won over any friends who didn't think they were dog people?**

..................................................................................
..................................................................................
..................................................................................
..................................................................................
..................................................................................
..................................................................................
..................................................................................
..................................................................................
..................................................................................
..................................................................................
..................................................................................
..................................................................................
..................................................................................
..................................................................................
..................................................................................
..................................................................................
..................................................................................
..................................................................................
..................................................................................
..................................................................................
..................................................................................
..................................................................................
..................................................................................
..................................................................................

**Out on the town: What are some of your pup's favorite dog-friendly neighborhood spots, shops, cafes?**

....................................................................................

....................................................................................

....................................................................................

....................................................................................

....................................................................................

....................................................................................

....................................................................................

....................................................................................

....................................................................................

....................................................................................

....................................................................................

....................................................................................

**Where would they love to go if they were allowed? The zoo? The cat café?**

..........................................................................................

..........................................................................................

..........................................................................................

..........................................................................................

..........................................................................................

..........................................................................................

..........................................................................................

..........................................................................................

..........................................................................................

..........................................................................................

..........................................................................................

..........................................................................................

..........................................................................................

..........................................................................................

..........................................................................................

..........................................................................................

..........................................................................................

..........................................................................................

..........................................................................................

..........................................................................................

..........................................................................................

..........................................................................................

..........................................................................................

..........................................................................................

**Stage a fun photo shoot for your dog. Use props or dramatic lighting.**

Here are the best shots!

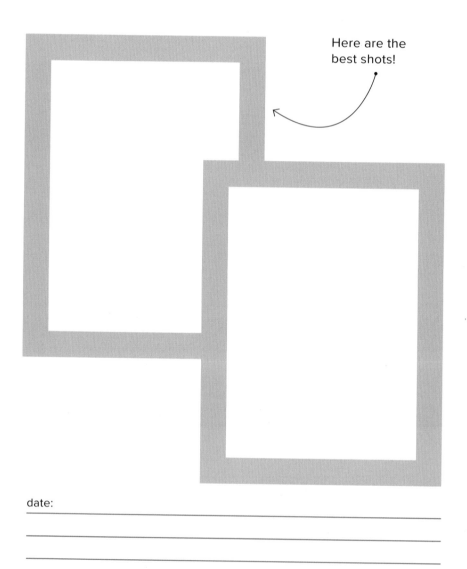

date: _____

_____

_____

_____

_____

# "The dog is the perfect portrait subject. He doesn't pose. He isn't aware of the camera."

– Patrick Demarchelier

# Write a letter to your dog.

Dear:

# "You know, a dog can snap you out of any kind of bad mood that you're in faster than you can think of."

— Jill Abramson

# Guestbook

Have your dog's friends, fans, and admires share
their favorite memories and stories of your pup.

name: _____ date: _____

favorite memory: _____

_____

_____

_____

_____

_____

_____

_____

_____

_____


name: _____ date: _____

favorite memory: _____

_____

_____

_____

_____

_____

_____

_____

_____

_____

name:                                                    date:

favorite memory:

_____
_____
_____
_____
_____
_____
_____
_____
_____
_____
_____

name:                                                    date:

favorite memory:

_____
_____
_____
_____
_____
_____
_____
_____
_____

name:                                    date:

favorite memory:

name:                                    date:

favorite memory:

145

name: _____ date: _____

favorite memory: _____
_____
_____
_____
_____
_____
_____
_____
_____
_____
_____
_____

name: _____ date: _____

favorite memory: _____
_____
_____
_____
_____
_____
_____
_____
_____
_____

name:                                    date:

favorite memory:

name:                                    date:

favorite memory:

name:                                      date:

favorite memory:

_____

_____

_____

_____

_____

_____

_____

_____

_____

_____

_____


name:                                      date:

favorite memory:

_____

_____

_____

_____

_____

_____

_____

_____

_____

_____

_____

name:                                      date:
_____      _____

favorite memory:
_____

_____

_____

_____

_____

_____

_____

_____

_____

_____

_____

name:                                      date:
_____      _____

favorite memory:
_____

_____

_____

_____

_____

_____

_____

_____

_____

_____

_____

_____

name:                                          date:

favorite memory:

_____

_____

_____

_____

_____

_____

_____

_____

_____

_____

_____


name:                                          date:

favorite memory:

_____

_____

_____

_____

_____

_____

_____

_____

_____

_____

_____

_____

name: _____          date: _____

favorite memory: _____

_____
_____
_____
_____
_____
_____
_____
_____
_____
_____
_____
_____
_____

name: _____          date: _____

favorite memory: _____

_____
_____
_____
_____
_____
_____
_____
_____
_____
_____
_____
_____
_____

name: _____    date: _____

favorite memory: _____

_____
_____
_____
_____
_____
_____
_____
_____
_____
_____

name: _____    date: _____

favorite memory: _____

_____
_____
_____
_____
_____
_____
_____
_____
_____
_____
_____
_____
_____

name: _____  date: _____

favorite memory: _____
_____
_____
_____
_____
_____
_____
_____
_____
_____
_____
_____

name: _____  date: _____

favorite memory: _____
_____
_____
_____
_____
_____
_____
_____
_____
_____
_____
_____

name: _____     date: _____

favorite memory: _____
_____
_____
_____
_____
_____
_____
_____
_____
_____
_____
_____

name: _____     date: _____

favorite memory: _____
_____
_____
_____
_____
_____
_____
_____
_____
_____
_____
_____

name: _____     date: _____

favorite memory: _____

_____
_____
_____
_____
_____
_____
_____
_____
_____
_____
_____
_____

name: _____     date: _____

favorite memory: _____

_____
_____
_____
_____
_____
_____
_____
_____
_____
_____
_____
_____
_____
_____

name:                                             date:

favorite memory:

name:                                             date:

favorite memory:

name: _____          date: _____

favorite memory: _____
_____
_____
_____
_____
_____
_____
_____
_____
_____
_____

name: _____          date: _____

favorite memory: _____
_____
_____
_____
_____
_____
_____
_____
_____
_____
_____
_____
_____
_____

name: _____ date: _____

favorite memory: _____

_____

_____

_____

_____

_____

_____

_____

_____

_____

_____

_____

name: _____ date: _____

favorite memory: _____

_____

_____

_____

_____

_____

_____

_____

_____

_____

_____

_____

Inspiring | Educating | Creating | Entertaining

Brimming with creative inspiration, how-to projects, and useful information to enrich your everyday life, quarto.com is a favorite destination for those pursuing their interests and passions.

10 9 8 7 6 5 4 3 2 1

Chartwell titles are also available at discount for retail, wholesale, promotional, and bulk purchase. For details, contact the Special Sales Manager by email at specialsales@quarto.com or by mail at The Quarto Group, Attn: Special Sales Manager, 100 Cummings Center Suite 265D, Beverly, MA 01915, USA.

ISBN: 978-0-7858-4209-5

Publisher: Wendy Friedman
Senior Managing Editor: Meredith Mennitt
Senior Design Manager: Michael Caputo
Designer: Sue Boylan

Printed in China